Waking Spirit
Prose & Poems the Spirit Sings

Shirley Cheng

Foreword by New York Times Bestselling Author, Cynthia Brian

Dance with Your Heart! Publishing
www.DanceWithYourHeart.com

Wappingers Falls, New York

Copyright © 2007 by Shirley Cheng

ISBN-13: 978-0-6151-3680-6
Library of Congress Control Number: 2006910623

This title is also available in hardback with the ISBN 978-0-6151-3893-0

www.DanceWithYourHeart.com
Wappingers Falls, New York, United States of America

All rights reserved by the author, Shirley Cheng. No part of this publication may be reproduced, stored in a retrieval system, or transmitted in any form or by any means, electronic, mechanical, photocopying, recording or otherwise, without the prior written permission of Shirley Cheng.

Mom's Choice Awards Winner

To the dearest, most beloved jewel that has ever been bestowed upon me by Heavenly Father: my wonderful mother Juliet Cheng, the cornerstone and light of my life; the foundation of my happiness, strength, and success. Thank you, Mom, for giving me such a wonderful life!

Many songs have been left unsung, their tales all untold. The melodies were never formed, with words all but spoken. Do not let the same misfortune befall your spirit. Sing your song while it is young. Let your melodies travel far and wide, and when you do, prepare to embrace the sky.

Table of Contents

Foreword by Cynthia Brian 13

Dance with Your Heart: How to Befriend Your Heart and the World around You 17

Midnight Dancers 23

Nightingale in Air 25

Nightingale's Melodies 25

Forget-Me-Nots in Reminiscence 25

Dance of Silvery Swans 26

Delighting Ripples 26

Yellow Shadows 26

Heart of Songs 27

Dove Love Song 29

Forest Melodies 29

Dance of Frozen Flowers 29

Let me Borrow Those Wings 30

Stormy Clouds' Snack 32

White Wings 32

Up, Down, All About 32

Flying Splendor..33

Intertwining Vines...33

Black Capes...33

Celebrate Your Existence, for It Is Your
Privilege!..34

Sunny Was Your Smile......................................39

Blanket of Cherry Blossoms..............................41

Blooming Dandelions..41

Mud Bath...41

Sunflowers' Hello..42

A Woodpecker's Visit..42

Chuckling Hyenas..42

Where the Valley Glows....................................43

Job of the Sun..44

Ruby Blossoms..44

The Downcast Willow..44

The Treasure Collector......................................45

Silky Threads...46

Art of Icicles..46

Bursting Buds..46

The Eye 47

Dancing Grand Ballet 47

Life in Shell 47

I'm Not Disabled—I'm Ultra-Abled 49

Thy Silvery Ladder 62

Thunderous March 63

Little Joey's Ride 63

New Pair of Wings 63

Ant Army 64

Pride of Lions 64

Frolicking Frog 64

The Moonlight Soiree 65

The Misty Moonlight 67

Flirting Diamonds 67

Awaiting Owls 67

Ivory Beauty 68

Full Moon's Blessing 69

Flickering Moonbeams 69

Leaves of Sunset Hues 69

Moonlight Embellishment 71

Crescent Yellow Moons 71

The Reflection 71

Thank You, O, Holy One! 72

Our Rewarding Gold 76

Survival Ball 77

Tropical Love 77

Gliding Eagles 77

Running on Water 78

Awakening Leaves 78

Peeking Orange Head 78

Waking Spirit 79

Beyond the Seashores 81

Morning Dove 81

Fiery Dance 81

The Inner Box 82

Blood-Red Hourglass 83

Laughing Dolphins 83

Blue Flaunt 83

Night Cats 84

Black Beauty 84

White Beauty	84
Those Unforgettable 180 Days	86
Sing Me a Song	92
Happy Winds	94
White Umbrellas	94
Shimmering Feathers	94
Crystalline Flowers	95
Upside Down Meals	95
Veil of Willows	95
The Summer Breeze	96
Midsummer's Blue Sky	97
Love on Midsummer's Nights	97
Wrath of Nature	97
Where the Old Oak Stands	98
Tumbling Leaves	99
The Red Silver Fir	99
Meadow of Cotton Balls	99
Praying Mantis	100
Red, Orange Leaves	100
Playful Rays	100

The Jewel from Heavenly Father	101
With You by My Side	105
Glorious Stars	106
Black and White Pair	106
Silly Peek-A-Boo	106
Veil of Waterfalls	107
Tumbling Waterfalls	107
Wing Dance	107
Twilight Serenade	108
Twilight Greeting	110
Midnight Ghostly Lights	110
Sleepy Spells	110
That Secretive Grin	111
Weeping Ocean	112
Moaning Winds	112
Seashell Sighing	112
Withering White	113
Kiss of King Cobra	113
Guilty Mockingbirds	113
The School People Crave	114

Will I Still Feel It?	118
Cool April Showers	119
Rain's Masterpiece	119
Shameless Rooster	119
Hunger of Venus Flytrap	120
Darting Blue Shadows	120
Ocean Sighs	120
When Your Spirit Is Blue	121
Hot Pink Flamingo	123
Festive Motif	123
Migrating V	123
Awake!	124
Tickle Me Not	125
Lullaby Whistle	125
Sliding in Tuxedos	125
Rise!	126
About the Author	128
Spotlight Reviews	133

Foreword

**By Cynthia Brian,
New York Times Best Seller**

Whenever I'm having a bad day, I think of Shirley Cheng! I had the pleasure of meeting Shirley during a radio show I produced when she was a guest for her three books, *Daring Quests of Mystics*; *The Revelation of a Star's Endless Shine: A Young Woman's Autobiography of a 20-Year Tale of Trials & Tribulations*; and *Dance with Your Heart: Tales and Poems That the Heart Tells*, all of which were written at age twenty. When I first received her pitch to be on the program, I was shocked to learn that she was just twenty-two years of age, blind, disabled, and had written her books using a screen reader called Jaws then typing with just two index fingers. Her tagline to me read:

"Although I'm blind, I can see far and wide; even though I'm disabled, I can climb high mountains. Let the ropes of hope haul you high!"

Wow! I was impressed. Of course I wanted to interview someone who appeared to be indefatigable. Could she be for real? I had to find out for myself. From the moment I welcomed her on the airwaves, her bubbly personality captured my delight. I could feel her smiles across the miles. Here was a young lady filled with faith, determined to make a difference and obviously having a blast living in the moment. She didn't sound incapacitated or helpless. She was a beacon of confidence, a role model of trusting in her Higher Power. The interview was a smash hit with listeners! Her optimism, outgoing nature, and obvious appreciation at being alive empowered us all to reach for the stars while expecting to land on them regardless of the obstacles standing in our path.

In her newest book, *Waking Spirit: Prose and Poems the Spirit Sings*, Shirley once again shares the joys of living. You are treated to dancing hearts, singing souls, and warm blanket of love wrapping around you with her use of poetry, spiritual prose, and haiku. Original quotes penned by Shirley are sprinkled throughout her writings as you engage in *A Moment with Shirley*.

Waking Spirit celebrates life while encouraging us all to appreciate what we already have. It's a book of survival, a tome of devotion, a bible of being.

I am especially impressed with the relationship between Shirley and her mother. They are best friends, one another's head cheerleaders, and soul comrades in the shuffle of reality. How many mother/daughter teams do you know that truly love and respect one another? If we could all just implement one lesson from these remarkable women, our world would be a more loving and peaceful place.

If Ms. Cheng's mother has been her guide on the side, God has been her sage on the stage. She is swift to give thanks for the many blessings and gifts bestowed upon her. Shirley is most grateful for the precious jewels of wisdom, wit, and whimsy that surround her, including her ability to communicate her affection for her Creator. One would not expect such a positive upbeat attitude from a girl who has suffered such enormous pain and formidable challenges throughout her life. Yet without those stumbling blocks and her deep faith in the goodness of her Heavenly Father, we would not have been graced with this soulful manuscript from this very talented young lady.

The book you are holding in your hands is a celebration of the dance of life. Awake your spirit, embrace the unknown, love unconditionally, and fan your flames of passion.

We have only one life in this body. Whether we are disabled or ultra-abled, we have the ability and the responsibility to treat our temples of our vitality with dignity and joy. Life is a banquet. Enjoy the buffet. Serve yourself a big helping of Shirley Cheng's inspiration and you'll be motivated to shoot for the stars.

And as Shirley is fond of saying, "Don't live each day as though it is your last; live each day as though it is your first." Today is the beginning of a stellar journey. Sit back, relax, and rise to sing your song with *Waking Spirit*. There is no quiet desperation here—only sensational courage and astounding beauty. Embrace your Godliness. You are a wonder of creation. Shine on! You are a STAR!

Cynthia Brian is a New York Times best selling author (her books include Be the Star You Are!, The Business of Show Business, Chicken Soup for the Gardener's Soul, Miracle Moments*), TV/radio personality and motivational speaker. She is available as an media/writing/acting coach.*
Contact www.star-style.com, or 925-377-STAR.

Dance with Your Heart

How to Befriend Your Heart and the World around You

First published in 101 Great Ways to Improve Your Life, Volume 2, *along with highly acclaimed experts like Jack Canfield, Dr. John Gray, Dr. Richard Carlson, Alan Cohen, and Bob Proctor*

What do you see when people dance? Is it how their hands and feet move so gracefully in such unison with one another, yet each of them sparkles with individuality? Are the dancers smiling? What does that mean? They may be joyous when they move their bodies to the rhythms of the music, but that is not all. They smile because they are dancing with their hearts.

What do I mean when I say they dance with their hearts? When you are dancing with your heart, you are dancing together with your heart and dancing using your heart, and as a result, you are becoming a dancing heart.

What do you feel when you see them dance? Do you feel like dancing as well? When you dance, you will project how you feel and what you feel onto any onlookers, causing them to have a desire, a need, to mirror your feelings, then finally your actions. You set good examples of life when you dance; you are teaching true things of life, so you must lead others by dancing yourself.

To dance with your heart, you must be pure. Release all the negative feelings hammering inside you and block out the ugly voices the outside world whispers stealthily in your ears. Become friends with yourself. What qualities do you look for in a friend?

Are you ready to become your own friend and dance with your heart? Take the following dance steps on your own before you can hold hands with your heart.

- Acceptance. Accept who you are as a whole. Accept how you feel. Accept how you think. Accept how you look from your head to your toes. You may not like to accept yourself as you are now because you feel you are not perfect. But what is perfection anyway? Is nature perfect? If so, then you must be perfect, too. Take a look—I bet that tall tree in your backyard has at least one torn branch, but is it still majestic? Does it still deserve to be called beautiful? Perfect?
- Openness. Be open, truthful, and honest with yourself. Do not lie to yourself. Do not live with pretense. When something is making you unhappy, face it, do not run away from it. Change the situation with a clear and honest

look. By closely examining the situation you are in, you will be able to find the root of the problem and plug it out. By remaining in the dark, you will never find that root, so turn on the lights!
- Understanding. Understand your feelings, thoughts, and why you behave the way you do. Find the purpose to your actions. Learn from your past and those situations that did not go as smoothly as hoped, and utilize what you learn to make your future bright.
- Love and appreciation. Love yourself. Honestly tell yourself, "I know I am not a bad person. I know I do my best in everything I do, and I know I am being my best, so I love myself because I am a good person with good intentions." Appreciate what you have and whom you have. Appreciate what you are able to do.
- Positivity. Count your blessings. Focus on the good things you do have at the present and the positive side of things. Do not dwell on bad situations, but instead, move forward and have

a bright attitude and outlook for the future. You have the ability to make a positive difference to your future just by being positive. Choosing the road to positivity and happiness will give you the strength, the desire, and the motivation to take giant steps forward. Don't pick the road to misery—it will just glue you to one spot, and you wouldn't want to get the glue onto others, now would you?

- Passion. Be passionate about who you are and what you do. Value life; cherish every minute that is given to you. Hold on tightly to the happy moments and their memories because when they're gone, they're gone forever. Live with conviction; live with vitality.
- Happiness. Smile often. Smile to yourself, even if there's no good reason. Smiling will warm you up, even when the days seem dreary. Frequently treat yourself to a big smile while working or frolicking; it is the sweetest treat you can give yourself, and the best part is that there are no calories!

Once you achieve calm in your soul, you will be able to spiritually connect with your own self from deep within you, and that is where your heart lies.

What is your heart? No, it is not the muscular organ that pumps blood through your body; it is your essence, your higher self or energy. No one has the power to harm your heart, especially if you don't allow outside negativity to pollute your spirit like a thick fog.

When you twirl and swirl with your heart, you will be sharply aware of all beauties of the world, things that you had not noticed or given heed to when you were not dancing with your heart. With the dance within you, you will have a broader sense of acceptance of who you are, and therefore your acceptance of others and the world around you will grow and grow to the point that you are spiritually connected with the entire universe—every creation breathes into you and you into it, fusing everything into one.

You will feel awake and alert when you waltz with your heart. Once you start dancing, you will not want to stop because the feeling will be too good and too powerful to let go, and you will crave it when you stop dancing. You will feel at peace with yourself and with the world. You will feel friendly toward those who follow in your dance steps or even toward those who abandon your dance to be lured into darkness.

When you dance, you will feel alive and free and painless, even if your body shouts of old age. Your body will grow older, but your essence will stay as young as a newly blossomed flower, but only with much more wisdom and understanding. Your dance will never grow old with age; instead, it will grow younger and wiser as each day passes for you will connect with all surrounding power to recharge your own energy.

Do I dance with my heart? You bet I do! Many joints in my body have been disfigured by severe juvenile rheumatoid arthritis since infancy, yet my heart dances freely and openly with no restraint. As we dance, my heart tells me all that it sees, so my blindness miserably fails to make me trip on my own feet.

Thus crank up the music, take my hand in yours, and let us dance with our hearts!

Midnight Dancers

Under the velvety night
Amid the bright spotlight
In the silence, leaves stir
Among the red silver fir
Little hearts awake
Their spirits cannot forsake
Their nightly delight
Under the bright moonlight

A circle forms
As silence transforms
Darkness does not deter
These young connoisseurs
Their waking spirits aglow
Wings beating to songs long ago
From their hearts, music flows
Of notes only they can bestow

Trees whistle, mixing in their song
The dance quickens, for it won't be for too long
Twirling in the sky, their wings spread out
All around, they dance about
Lingering to one long lasting song
Before the last light is gone
Gently, the moon bids farewell
As the last note ends in a fare-thee-well

A Moment with Shirley

Be your own true best friend
and you will become a true
best friend of the world.

Nightingale in Air

Nightingale in air
Singing songs soothing and light
Love resides within

Nightingale's Melodies

Nightingale in flight
Making merry melodies
Creates memories

Forget-Me-Nots in Reminiscence

Forget-me-nots sway
In reminiscence of love
Tenderly forgive

Dance of Silvery Swans

Silvery swans dance
Gracefully stretching long necks
Spread lily-white wings

Delighting Ripples

Ripples delight when
Willows tickle blue waters
Into laughing streams

Yellow Shadows

Yellow shadows moon
Casts, breaking through stormy clouds
Before lightning strikes

Heart of Songs

In the heart of songs the spirit wakes
Quivering with hope for a life brand new
Sunshine to bring days afresh
And waters to wash away all of blue

The notes from the heart they flow
Sensations of all wonders it sings
The delicate grandness the melodies bring
For all young hearts to sing aglow

A Moment with Shirley

Hope builds strong wings, so let your hopes bloom to lift you high and discover the true bliss of life.

Dove Love Song

Love eternally
Flows joyously from its heart
White dove gaily sings

Forest Melodies

Melodies hover
Over forest fineries
Leaves clap in a dance

Dance of Frozen Flowers

White frozen flowers
Dance in gray skies carried by
Invisible arms

Let me Borrow Those Wings

O, fly to wondrous places
The wind shall take thee to undiscovered spaces
Where hearts are dancing to songs of delight
Sung by the spirits of light

Oh, let me borrow those wings
With them, I shall soar up high
Till my young heart does a swing
And through my lips escapes a sigh

There are valleys I long to see
Where flowers and trees live on love
Sprinkled by the honey of bees
Caressed by the gentle wings of white doves

O, fly to wondrous places
The wind shall take thee to undiscovered spaces
Where hearts are dancing to songs of delight
Sung by the spirits of light

On my journey, my spirit shall sing
To forget the darkness left behind
Enchanting melodies, my heart will bring
The notes harmonious, delicately intertwined

In that land, I shall gather up the sunshine
The magic, wonders, I will collect
These treasures for all, not just mine
Then homebound I shall fly with all respect

O, fly to wondrous places
The wind shall take thee to undiscovered spaces
Where hearts are dancing to songs of delight
Sung by the spirits of light

With the wings, my dreams will render true
Those delights I long to bring
For my home folks to live anew
So, may I borrow those wings?

O, fly to wondrous places
The wind shall take thee to undiscovered spaces
Where hearts are dancing to songs of delight
Sung by the spirits of light

Stormy Clouds' Snack

Stormy clouds munching
On round yellow moon, leaving
A half-eaten cheese

White Wings

White wings flap freely
Soaring amid cloudless skies
Touching grand heavens

Up, Down, All About

Rotating each wing
The hummingbird darts up, down
backwards, it speeds off

Flying Splendor

Soar over highlands
Fly into puffy cottons
Swanning above seas

Intertwining Vines

Intertwining vines
Slithering up thick tree trunks
Snaking between limbs

Black Capes

Bats spreading black capes
Fluttering in darkest caves
In the depths of night

Celebrate Your Existence, for It Is Your Privilege!

Also published in Wake Up...Live the Life You Love: Finding Your Life's Passion, Second Edition, *together with contributions by Dr. Wayne Dyer, Anthony Robbins, and Brian Tracy*

Do you love life unconditionally? Do you accept and cherish days that are dark and dreary rather than light-filled? Has your passion for life died away when life seems to play games which you lose?

It is easy to love life when you achieve what you desire. You embrace life when things go right. But what if when life throws you stones when you least expect it? How do you feel when, at times, life seems to turn its back on you? If you suddenly lost your eyesight, would you still feel passionate and continue to see past the loss and look into a bright future, and cherish the privilege of what you had in the past?

I love life unconditionally, and the flames of my passion will never die. Yes, I am passionately, madly in love with life and, I know, it loves me unconditionally in return. But how, you must wonder, could it love me unconditionally when it has snatched my eyesight away, leaving me to yearn for sight of the stars I can now only wish upon?

For seventeen years, I had the honor of beholding the beauty of our world; I experienced the sheer pleasure of seeing my mother's smile alight upon her eyes; I delighted in treating my soul to breathtaking scenes of nature: celestial diamonds, the green velvet that blankets our Earth, and the glistening mirrors that winter creates upon our ponds; and now, I have lovingly tucked these photographs in my mind, and I am still able to enjoy them in my heart, from which I continue to see the world. I do not scorn life for taking away my ability to see; instead, I am grateful for having owned this gift before.

When you fall in love with someone, do you fall in love with a perfect person? No, because that person does not exist. Instead, you love that person for who he or she is and how he or she makes you feel. Thus it is, with life: acknowledge the times when you have lost and be grateful for the times you have won. Unlike an imperfect lover, life will never abandon you; for better, for worse, for richer, for poorer, in sickness or in health, the sun rays will never leave your side.

Knowing this, I am passionate about being alive and returning life's love with an intensity that matches the power of fire. My heart dances whenever I think about my existence.

But what is being alive really? Being alive is having the privilege to smile, laugh, taste, and touch. It is having the ability to smell the special scent your mother carries; to run with the wind; and to dance with your heart.

Without life, how can you know the delight of waking up to the songs of birds or dancing to the rhythms of the ocean? How can you see the beautiful arch across the sky after a refreshing rain? And how can you have the chance to taste your salty teardrops on your lips?

Your existence gives you priceless treasures: the full spectrum of emotions; the sharing of feelings; your talents, ideas, and imagination; and countless other riches of the universe. You are indeed immeasurably rich, much richer than the infinite unborn souls.

True, not all the jewels of your existence shine and shimmer; many of them are steep mountains you must climb and deep oceans you must cross, but these challenges and obstacles are the jewels that make you stronger. Challenges are life's vaccines: they exercise your spirit to help you withstand high winds and equip your soul with the necessary tools to battle future storms.

I have received many of these vaccines; the obstacles have left numerous scars on my body in all shapes and sizes, but these marks have made me stronger and more invincible as I wait for the next high mountain to scale. I relish the taste of victory each and every time I battle and win. If there were no challenges, how could I name myself a victor? If there were no darkness, how could the stars appear so bright?

Be thankful for the gems that sparkle; focus on the gifts your existence has bestowed upon you. Do not let any dust or dirt tarnish the value of these diamonds; the dirt itself cannot touch or harm the treasures—only you have the power to ultimately soil the gems, so handle them with grace and appreciation. For each day that passes, thank for that day and its riches. Instead of waiting for disaster to strike in order to be thankful for what little is left after its devastation, love and appreciate everything and everyone right now.

I embrace my existence with my whole heart and soul, and I accept all the jewels—the bright, along with the not-so bright—my life has granted me. I cherish my existence and everything else it encompasses, knowing that I can create more wondrous treasures by using what I have. Although I'm blind, I can see far and wide, as my heart tells me all it sees; even though I'm disabled, I can climb high mountains, for my spirit soars with the wind, unafraid to face any rain and hail. In spite of all the high mountains I have climbed, I have arrived at each and every top with a smile. I have conquered thorny jungles and fiery seas and come out with stars in my arms. I am able to achieve all this, for I count my blessings every day, knowing that there is always someone out there who is in a much worse situation than I, so I am thankful for what I have and who is around me.

Some souls let their troubles veil the gems, so they are unable to treasure the diamonds. Do not let the same misfortune befall you. When you are given life, hold on to it tightly yet delicately; cherish what has been given to you: your privilege to enjoy dawn's first rays, your power to give words of comfort to a stranger, and your fortune to receive warm embraces after a good cry. If you allow your mishaps to cloud these treasures—or do not realize the true value of challenges—you will make your situation worse than it already is, losing every good thing you do have. And watch out for the thieves who try to belittle your gifts; they are the people who refuse to recognize the worth of life.

What would you have missed if your existence had never existed?

I know I am able to laugh; I am able to weep. Without my life, I would be able to do none of these. Thus, let us celebrate our existences together and return life's unconditional love; let us rejoice over the beauty of our treasures, and embrace all of our days!

Sunny Was Your Smile

Sunny was your smile
In sweet reminiscence
Of oceans that stretched for miles
Treating delights to all senses

White wings fluttered
Yonder the shore of blue waters
As waves billowed in great dances
Playing with its life down under

Rays caressed the foamy flowers
Turning all into celestial diamonds
And warmed the isles of golden towers
Built by the owners of laughing voices

But after that dark night passed
Veiling your windows to the world
The light can no longer shine through
Yet sunny is your smile still
In sweet reminiscence
Of oceans that stretched for miles
Treating delights to all senses

A Moment with Shirley

Do not leave out any one color
life has given you to create
your painting.

Blanket of Cherry Blossoms

Cherry blossoms fall
Tenderly atop bird nests
Blanketing younglings

Blooming Dandelions

Dandelions bloom
Amid bright meadows sprinkled
With shining dewdrops

Mud Bath

Rolling in the mud
The fat pig squeals in delight
To be squeaky clean

Sunflowers' Hello

Sunflowers turning
To their grandmother above
Nodding a hello

A Woodpecker's Visit

Knock, knock, knock; who's there?
The wooden home vibrates from
A woodpecker's call

Chuckling Hyenas

Hyenas chuckle
Teasing the silvery moon
Saliva dripping

Where the Valley Glows

Let us fly far away
To where the valley glows
With love as blossoming buds
Sprinkled by drops of honey dew

We shall discover chests overflowing
Of all wondrous of sensations
Happiness never overdue
But plenty to stretch on end

Thus take my hand in yours
Spread our wings we shall
Find the land within
Hidden with as yet to be discovered gems

Job of the Sun

Smiling, the sun peeks
Over horizons, peeling
Away the darkness

Ruby Blossoms

Ruby blossoms flow
Downstream where lovers sigh to
Beating of their hearts

The Downcast Willow

The downcast willow
Sorrowfully weeps for love
Of days long ago

The Treasure Collector

I hear laughter in my heart
For the wind has blown me a kiss
To add to my work of art
So none shall plummet into the abyss

I collect treasures sent my way
Of ones life picked out with care
And could never cause a frown of dismay
Delights of the common and rare

Thus, if a gem you decide to leave
Do not forget about me
For my collection hungers for more
Of all that life grants forevermore

Silky Threads

Silky threads shimmer
Bedecked with April showers
Seductively lure

Art of Icicles

Melting icicles
Dimly paint spectrum upon
Frozen white blankets

Bursting Buds

Bright buds burst freely
Amid open green grasslands
Waving heavenward

The Eye

Winds blow in fury
Trees twist, dust flies; then silence
The eye has arrived

Dancing Grand Ballet

Standing on tip toes
Dressed in white decked with red crowns
Cranes dance grand ballet

Life in Shell

Snuggled in its shell
A tiny heart stirs, pecking
Freedom, it longs so

A Moment with Shirley

Don't live each day as though it is your last; live each day as though it is your first.

I'm Not Disabled—I'm Ultra-Abled

The baby, her large dark eyes aglow, laughed gleefully as the smiling admirers looked on. Her mother lovingly scooped her up into her arms and turned to the few women, clad in white, who were eyeing the infant girl. "Let me carry Happy Baby," requested one of the women, opening her arms. As she had many times before, the mother placed her baby in the woman's arms. "She is always so happy, this Happy Baby," the woman cooed as others smiled in agreement.

Indeed, this thirteen-month-old child was always happy, laughing and pointing at everyday objects whenever her eyes met something that delighted her senses as if she knew nothing of pain. Yet, in truth, her tiny body was crippled, and just merely a month ago, she had knocked on death's door; her stiff joints were swollen, and pain often took over her like a knife cutting through her soul.

Being confined in this dismal hospital room, with nurses and doctors in white uniforms going hither and thither, would veil many spirits with dark clouds, but it failed to turn Happy Baby's smile upside down. Despite the severe juvenile rheumatoid arthritis ravaging within her, she smiled whenever she could, many times through tears of constant pain. There were days during which she could not sit up or move a single muscle. Seeing her daughter near her deathbed, and knowing that American hospitals offered no medicine other than aspirin (which only worsened her condition), the mother brought her daughter to Shanghai, China, her native country, to seek treatment, and that was where I received my nickname of Happy Baby twenty-two years ago.

Although I do not remember those early times as my mother Juliet Cheng brokenheartedly watched me cry in pain, I do recall the times when I, at two years of age, laughed through my tears. I remember excitedly pointing at a pretty fabric in the room while crying my little heart out as every cell in my body screamed in agony.

Before my fourth birthday, I had traveled to China for the third time, seeking the right treatment that could lessen my suffering, and ultimately save my life from the grasp of death. Once in China, at age four, I was finally able to walk while receiving effective shots combined with massage therapy. For the first time, I explored a world I had never really known: the world outside of hospital walls. I was fascinated by everything I saw, heard, and touched, experiencing the new feelings that come with walking, running, and dancing. I caught bugs of all shapes and sizes, ranging from black spiders to bumble bees — none scared me — and studied them intensively. I tasted the freedom of discovery that I never knew existed. I felt alive as I chased after butterflies and picked wildflowers alongside the hospital where I was hospitalized.

But sadly, my walking days ended a year later when the quality of the shots went downhill; but my high spirit did not leave me. I continued to admire the outside world through my hospital or home windows, daydreaming of those good old days I would hopefully be able to relive again.

My passion for life has always lived in me, although I did not give it much thought when I was young; I simply enjoyed life without stopping to think about it. As I grew older, I realized that life was simply too precious to be wasted. I was given life, I must cherish it. I marvel at the beauties and wonders of life. Through every crystalline snowflake that falls from the sky and from every song a bird trills, I experience a miracle. I cannot help but be empowered by life to live, to enjoy being alive, and to experience what life has to offer.

Life is full of love; I feel love emitting from every crevice and corner of the world. I experience love when I smile, touch, and taste; I know love whenever sunrays kiss my hair while gentle breezes playfully tease it in a dance. How could I not love life back?

Without life, how could I have known the delight of dancing to the rhythms of the winds? How could I experience the sheer pleasure of exchanging warm embraces with loved ones? And if it had not been for my existence, how could I know how powerful love feels and how precious it is to be loved back?

I have experienced love all of my life, both from the infinite love my beloved mother endlessly provides me and from the love I experience from living.

Thus, I have never given up, not after years of unimaginable pain, traveling from one country to another, moving from one hospital to another, receiving one disappointment after another, and not even when I nearly drowned twice in seas of darkness, once when I was less than two years of age and once at age seven. Each time, my primary source of love and security was suddenly snatched away from me: my mother, who has been the cornerstone and light of my life. She lost custody of me twice in America after disagreeing with doctors' recommended treatments—treatments that would have ended my young life. She said no to the doctors, and they took me out of her loving arms and trapped me inside their gloomy hospital rooms in order to force the unwanted, harmful treatments on me. But I kept my hopes high as I knew my mother held reason in her hands, and with this, she would win me back; justice would prevail. Her love for me conquers all, and she has this invincible stamina to fight for my life till she wins.

Indeed, I was back in her arms both times after months of fighting and numerous court sessions she had to attend. The last case in 1990 made international headlines; my mother appeared on *CBS This Morning* with Paula Zahn as she fought to save my life, gaining the support of celebrities and numerous doctors.

Those were the stormiest seas I have ever survived. I thank the spirit of my mother for having the strength to swim those seas with me and saving my life before I drowned. I had her, but what was her lifesaver? Her faith in Jehovah God, her power to never give up — it is from her, that I receive my strength.

I am an artist of life; I am the creator of my destiny and I choose which road I take. At every crossroads, I pick the path that leads to happiness. With every step I take, I admire what I encounter along the way.

Holding high prospects for wonderful outcomes, I have overcome every challenge I have faced, including starting school for the very first time in my life at age eleven where the language was foreign to me.

Owing to years of hospitalization between America and China, I did not receive any form of education until my health had finally been stabilized. Having been brought up in a single, Chinese-speaking family with no influence on education, I knew only the alphabets and very few simple English words. I knew that two plus two equals four and that three times five is fifteen; other than that, my book knowledge was nearly non-existent. How I yearned to read a book or write down what my heart longed to say! Every time I saw a yellow school bus pass by, I wished I were one of the students lucky enough to ride in it. It puzzled—and still puzzles—me why there are more frowns than smiles on many faces of students. There is so much that needs to be learned, probed, and discovered. How could I live without understanding the Earth where I call home? How could I not want to learn more about the elements that make up who I am?

Without the ability to capture what I felt in words, I portrayed all I beheld in my drawings. I brought ballerina cats and singing parakeets to life in my artwork and the crafts I made with my arthritic hands, hands with fingers that can't straighten and one that refuses to bend at all, so I always look as though I am pointing somewhere mysterious. But I have been told that they are "artistic hands," with long, pointy fingers.

At age eleven, after years of being stranded in hospital beds in America and China, at long last, I started schooling in a special education class in elementary school. I was highly excited about going to school for the very first time, and I rose from my bed that morning with high spirits. My first day of school glided by smoothly, and I instantly befriended my kind teacher and classmates, holding high gratitude in my heart for the teacher who would bring me one of the most precious gifts in life.

After returning home that day, I began my journey into reading with the simple picture book picked out by my teacher. I could not read a single sentence, so my mother went over each word with me. Within an hour or two, I was able to read nearly the entire book by myself with perfect pronunciation. I practiced reading the book for a few days until I made certain I could read every word with ease. Every day thereafter, I brought home a new book to read. Within the first few weeks of school, I had filled two notebooks with poetry, and shortly thereafter, I was reading at fourth-grade level. I was floating on cloud nine; no longer was I lying on my hospital bed daydreaming about school and reading—my dream had finally come true.

After about 180 days of attendance in elementary school (during which I went to China for the sixth and last time), I mastered grade level in all areas and entered a regular sixth grade class in middle school. I received numerous academic, art, and literary awards, including Student of the Year in sixth grade, Student of the Month in seventh grade, and an excellence award for achieving the highest grade of 97 in Earth science in the entire eighth grade class.

Connecting every large road, are many

smaller roads, extending outward like the tributaries of a river; and each road holds a new challenge I must face and conquer. At times, the challenges I encounter in the narrow, winding roads have been more difficult to navigate than those in the wider roads. Achieving what I was set out to accomplish in school was the easiest mountain to climb; battling ignorance and apathy of human nature were the darkest roads, with thorns that tried to tear my soul apart, but to no avail. I am made of life; my spirit is connected to the spirit of life, supplying my soul with the shield of light to ward off lurking shadows.

Every obstacle, every barrier, I have run into, have miserably failed to injure my spirit, including, at age seventeen, the latest turning-point stone life threw at me: the loss of my eyesight. Being an artist of the visual arts, it was a great loss for me; I miss immensely seeing the beauty of our world, although all that I have known and seen are tucked safely in my memory book, deep in my heart. I hold on tightly to the hope that I will someday behold the world again, but until that day comes, I do not stumble; instead, I dance gleefully, for my heart tells me all it sees as we glide far and wide.

Life is the power I use to live on, bringing me the strength and determination to take my giant steps forward. I do not look back in the sense of losing myself in the past; instead, I look forward to a bright future where a whole road awaits me that will bring me many surprises, and where I can fully experience the delight of living.

I did just that when my vision deteriorated during my sophomore year in high school. During that time, I learned only by listening to my teachers as they taught math, chemistry, and French, and yet, I still maintained A's.

I persisted when my eyesight completely forsook me. I had no choice but to stop attending school in April of tenth grade, and I received home-tutoring from the tutors my school sent. I completed all of my assignments strictly by using tape recorders, listening to the materials (e.g., homework, exams) and recording my answers and essays on cassette tapes from which my teachers graded me. I also successfully balanced and wrote long chemistry equations in my head without vision or Braille (I cannot use Braille because of my severe arthritis).

As much as I wanted to earn a diploma from my high school, I could not—I accumulated only half of the credits required to graduate (from these credits, however, I earned an overall average of 97, which is a GPA of 3.9, without any advanced placement classes)—so I earned my high school equivalency diploma instead. I took the GED exam, including mathematical calculations and problem solving, graphs, and an essay, without the aid of vision, and yet, I earned a special recognition award for receiving an exceptionally high score of 3280. I was a student speaker at my graduation ceremony, and was the only one who received a thunderous standing ovation after speaking.

Since I no longer could depict life's many fascinations through artwork, I turned to writing to express my thoughts and emotions, and to share with others my imagined worlds and creations. My passion for writing has existed within my soul since I was a young child. I have always been fascinated with pens and paper, for I know that these utensils portray so much in life through drawings and writings. These tools allow us to create and project our deep thoughts and emotions. Before receiving education, I used to hold a pen in my hand and scribble made-up words. How I yearned to write down what I felt; how I longed to relate to others, on paper, the little stories I had in my heart, and record the beauty my eyes beheld around me. I am a person who cherishes and appreciates life, and all it has to offer, from the largest stars in the heavens down to the tiniest living organism.

I began my career as a writer when I was twenty, and by the time I knew it, I had written three books within one year.

I am so thankful to live in times of technological advances, for a screen reader (computer software) has enabled me to become a writer when it would otherwise have been impossible. The reader tells me which keys I type and reads the text on the screen, except graphic text. Because of my arthritis, I can type only with my two index fingers, but I manage it quite well, typing at the speed of about sixty words per minute. Not only have I written the books entirely on my own, but I have also successfully completed every self-publishing task, including formatting my manuscripts, by myself. I also design and maintain my own website. Yes, a blind individual can do all that with plenty of passion and faith!

Every time I think about the past, it brings a smile to my face, even when I recollect the dark days, for my mother's spirit and mine have sought out the light amid every dark tunnel.

I see a long, rugged road ahead of me, but I am unafraid to follow it and persist onward. Instead, my soul tingles with excitement for every minute of the future. I have much more to achieve, to experience, to know; I have much to give, to show, to express; and only with an open heart can I achieve all that.

Life is like a dream full of mysteries, twists and turns. Like a detective, I keep my senses open for new opportunities to better appreciate, if not fathom, the unknown. I welcome every change in life and every chance life grants me so I can discover new avenues to explore. With each passing day, I eagerly await a new adventure; I yearn for more understanding of life and all of its complexities.

Without dreams, life would be a lonely, empty place, one with no hopes, feelings, and pursuits. I have built many bridges with dreams. I have crossed each and every one in my wheelchair, and will continue to build more as I journey through life.

No mountain is high enough to hold me back; no wind is strong enough to blow me down. There are stars I must reach; there are roads I must take, and with my mother's hand in mine, I spread my wings wide to take the flight I am destined to take.

I may be blind, I may be crippled, but I'm not disabled — I'm ultra-abled.

A Moment with Shirley

Why should the sky be the limit when the universe is grander?

Thy Silvery Ladder

Let down thy silvery ladder
Down to where the lonely land lies
Up the ladder I shall climb
With bag in hand to collect all that shines
A song I will sing as I journey high
To thy ivory lair, for my heart longs
To deck my world with thy glorious light

The world below lies dismal and bleak
Through the years, the happiness has fled
Aimlessly the darkness roams
Endlessly the silence flows
But the pain, I shall battle with nary a shudder
Till victory lies in my hand
With thy light as the savior of our world

Thunderous March

Earth trembles, dust flies
Thump, thump, thump; a gray band of
Elephants marching

Little Joey's Ride

Grass, trees, rocks hop by
Tiny joey enjoying
Rides in mother's pouch

New Pair of Wings

From a deep slumber
It awakes; a dainty pair
Of wings it now owns

Ant Army

One bone, an ant finds
Then crawls away; ten minutes
Pass, an army comes

Pride of Lions

Yonder bright meadows
Roams a pride of proud lions
Roaring mightily

Frolicking Frog

Hop, hop goes the frog
Springing among soft lilies
Plop! It disappears

The Moonlight Soiree

O, have you danced under the moon
Where the wind gently blows?
Few have danced to the lovely tunes
Of days forgotten long ago

Overhead, the silvery moon stands
A song the wind gently blows
To the melodies, I clap my hands
With notes in my heart, I sway to and fro

Under the spotlight, my dance has begun
The velvety curtains have drawn aside
Above me, diamonds twinkle one by one
Music flows from the windward side

My spirit awakens feeling grand
My heart sings along to the sighing wind
Whisking me into long forgotten lands
Holding all the pleasures I need no longer find

O, have you danced under the moon
Where the wind gently blows?
Few have danced to the lovely tunes
Of days forgotten long ago

The sweetness, I taste on my lips
Refreshing drops, I savor with each sip
Red roses adorning glassy tables
Along with all heart's desired delectable

Marble floors reflecting happy faces
Women in their finest silks and laces
Upon each bosom, a red rose is pinned
Their hair teased by the playful wind

Gentlemen bow low in honor
Their grace could be no finer
Kindness flow in harmonious waves
Betwixt these gentlemen of the brave

O, have you danced under the moon
Where the wind gently blows?
Few have danced to the lovely tunes
Of days forgotten long ago

Oh, how my heart longs to stay
Forever in this moonlight soiree
For the moment, these delights I must part, for
The next moon shall open the grand door

O, have you danced under the moon
Where the wind gently blows?
Few have danced to the lovely tunes
Of days forgotten long ago

The Misty Moonlight

The misty moonlight
Cloaks countryside lovingly
Mists gently stroking

Flirting Diamonds

Winking diamonds flirt
Adorned on velvety black
Gown; coyly smiling

Awaiting Owls

Eyes round as full moons
Owls silently await night
For midnight delights

Ivory Beauty

Up in your ivory tower
Under the starlit sky
Your beauty emits power
None could turn a blind eye

The silvery hair you let down
caresses the emptiness below
In your white evening gown
All in sight bow low

Celestial diamonds adorn your crown
Winking in mischief with no bounds
Your loveliness is never with a frown
As though youth is forever newfound

What's the secret of your vitality?
Is it love that creates your beauty?
Or happiness that rules your mentality?
Oh, whisper your secret, dear Ivory Beauty

Full Moon's Blessing

Full moon arises
Yonder quiet countryside
Blessing deep slumbers

Flickering Moonbeams

Moonbeams flickering
Atop shadows stealthily
Dosing sleepiness

Leaves of Sunset Hues

Leaves of sunset hues
Tumble over rocks, falling
Into whooshing streams

A Moment with Shirley

To love and accept life is to love and accept God.

Moonlight Embellishment

Moon embellishing
Silver wolves with glowing cloaks
Caressing softly

Crescent Yellow Moons

Crescent yellow moons
Hang in abundance on trees
Loved by all monkeys

The Reflection

High up, looking down
The giraffe touches noses
With its reflection

Thank You, O, Holy One!

This paean will be featured in Letters to God, *a book series created and compiled by Vicki R. Craig, Esq.*

Dear Heavenly Father:

My heart sings joyously with gratitude for You; how could it not when I have so much for which to be thankful? You, Loving Creator of all beauties and wonders, have given me countless riches in life. From everything You have created—from every crystalline flower and from every tune a bird whistles—I feel love overflowing from every crevice and corner. I experience love whenever I smile, touch, and taste; I know love when gentle breezes caress my face and whenever the sunrays kiss my hair.

Though my eyes have been veiled for six years, I do not scorn life for taking away my ability to see; instead, I am grateful for having owned this power before, as I know You work under mysterious plans, plans humans could not comprehend (although I fervently hope to someday better fathom the unknown). For seventeen years, I had the honor of beholding the beauty of Your creations. I experienced the sheer pleasure of seeing my mother's eyes twinkle with mischief; I had the delight of treating my soul to breathtaking scenes of nature: the diamonds that accentuate the beauty of the black velvet, glorious flowers that dance in the air, and the masterpiece rain paints against a clearing sky. And now, I have lovingly tucked these memories deep within my soul, from where I continue to see the world, for my heart shares with me all it sees.

And yet, God, above all things, the treasure I love most—one that surpasses even my own existence—is the one I have had before my birth into this world, and for this, my soul is full of the sincerest appreciation for You.

On the day my life began, You bestowed upon me this most precious jewel. This treasure has shone endless light upon me, bringing unconditional love, unwavering support, overflowing happiness, and the softest serenity to my life. I have never felt empty or alone, as I know this gem has me wrapped in its warm blanket, protecting me from the darkest corners of the world. Although twenty-three years have flown by, battling through wind and storms, its sublimity is undaunted, and not a speck of dust has ruined its beauty. It continues to shimmer, not flinching from dirt or mud. I always have it near me; if it is physically away, it is always locked safely in my heart.

Yes, Father, that diamond is indeed my beloved mother Juliet Cheng, a beautiful woman in every sense of the word. Together, my mother and I have shared laughter and tears; the best of times and the worst of times.

Through Your guiding light, we have fought as a team with our swords of justice. We have conquered fiery oceans and thorny jungles and come out with music in our hearts. She has climbed all the high mountains with me, supporting and encouraging me every step of the way. She has carried me on dangerous roads and saved my life numerous times from the grasp of death. I would have been long gone if it had not been for the invincible stamina and courage You gave her to fight for my life till she held victory in her hands.

As You know, my mother has done all this while battling her own horrendous illnesses. But she keeps moving forward, never abandoning me nor faltering in any way. This angel in disguise does everything in her power to keep me well and happy. Her love for me is "higher than the sky and deeper than the ocean." With her love always within me, I feel all the wonders of sensations. I am a billionaire though my pockets are empty. I have all the riches in the world: love, happiness, peace, security, and support. What more is there to life than those pearls of the universe? She is my life, and I give her all I can offer—my love, heart, and soul.

She and I can never be spiritually separated—we live within each other's hearts; if we are oceans away, we will still be near to each other. We are binary stars, ever revolving around each other, never drifting apart. She will never be absent of her fiery glow, and I will forever shine by her side. As long as there is life, there will be her love and mine.

Thus, God, our beloved Almighty, You have blessed my life with Your gift! As long as my soul is in existence, it lives on with high gratitude; for every day that passes, warmth embraces me as I am endlessly reminded of Your infinite love.

I thank You in the name of Jesus Christ. Amen.

Eternally gratefully,

Shirley Cheng

Our Rewarding Gold

Days would be darkest without you
Nights to lose their flavors, too
My dreams would be too few
All the happiness long overdue

Up the mountains we have gone
Across oceans we have swum
Beneath stormy clouds, flown our songs
Through hardships, into one we've become

By my side, we battle on end
Hand in hand, the power we hold
All the evils, we must fend
Each victory, our rewarding gold

Days would be darkest without you
Nights to lose their flavors, too
My dreams would be too few
All the happiness long overdue

Up ahead, thorny jungles await
Your heart in mine, I'll keep my head high
Long ago, we accepted our fate
Thus forward, we stride with not a sigh

Days would be darkest without you
Nights to lose their flavors, too
My dreams would be too few
All the happiness long overdue

Survival Ball

Rolling as one ball
Afloat flood waters, squirming
Ants survive flooding

Tropical Love

Tropic canopies
Shade a bird couple in love
Two hearts beat as one

Gliding Eagles

Gliding serenely
Engulfed within cotton balls
Eagles hover high

Running on Water

Hesitating not
The lizard steps on the pond
How it speeds across!

Awakening Leaves

Leaves hang suspended
Swaying to songs of spirits
Waking to new life

Peeking Orange Head

Peeking orange head
Descending 'neath horizons
Sun winks its goodbye

Waking Spirit

When dormant it lies
All sensations travel by
Kiss it gently on the brow
If you may, then sleepiness shall vow
No longer shall it yawn, for
Greatness has opened the door

Spirit, rise!
Prepare for a brand new day
In it, all the treasures suffice
Ready to be shared from day to day
Internally your essence shall glow
Thus, let your songs eternally flow

A Moment with Shirley

Many dream dreams; only a few create dreams.

Be the creator of your or someone else's dream!

Beyond the Seashores

Beyond the seashores
Far into the bubbly brine
Rays dance on waters

Morning Dove

Morning dove's soft coos
Greet grand smiling sun above
Bringing a new day

Fiery Dance

Orange hands reach out
Wildly waving to each breeze
Torching all they touch

The Inner Box

Open that door and what do you find?
Maybe plenty of junk and useless things
Pay no heed to those given by others
For they ruin your beauty and hide the treasures

Dig up that inner box
Find that key you had locked up
Perhaps it's under Misery and Despair
Brush away all the dirt and dust

Insert the key in the tiny hole
See all the jewels long forgotten?
Take them all and spread them out
Fill yourself up with Love and Happiness

There is plenty to share with others
So invite the world to a cup of tea
Lay Joy and Peace on the table
And let us not forget Understanding

Blood-Red Hourglass

Deep blood-red hourglass
Boldly the widow displays
Upon her blackness

Laughing Dolphins

Splashing clear waters
Silver dolphins laugh in glee
Creating bubbles

Blue Flaunt

Blue head held proudly
The peacock opens his tail
Twirling and flaunting

Night Cats

Dark as starless nights
Black cats stealthily creeping
In forgotten realms

Black Beauty

Long black mane flying
The black beauty gallops, its
Sun-kissed fur gleaming

White Beauty

Sporting purest white
The butterfly rests on a
Rose of white beauty

A Moment with Shirley

One who dares to be daring and listens to the voice from one's heart has the guts to enjoy the grandness of life.

Those Unforgettable 180 Days

"This is 'carrots,'" said my mother, pointing to the word that might as well be Russian or Arabic for all I knew. "Carrots," she repeated, then told me what the word means in Chinese, my native tongue.

"Carrots," I said after her.

"Perfect." She pointed to another word in the thin picture book adorned with a yellow cover. The pictures showed a boy planting his own garden. "This is 'pineapples.'"

I eagerly listened to each syllable as my mother pronounced each word clearly. So this was my first official day of learning how to read after attending my first day of school. No, I wasn't a chubby pre-schooler, nor was I a hyper kindergartner; in less than sixty days, I would blow out eleven candles on my birthday cake.

"I'm going to wash the dishes. I'll be back in a little bit to check on how you're getting along with the book." She gently touched my hair before she left the room.

I studied each sentence, flipping through the book and enjoying the pictures; not knowing how to read, I could only admire the talented drawings. I usually immersed myself in creating pictures of my own ever since I was about six or seven. I turned back to the first page of the book, which had been chosen by my special education teacher. I felt a tingling in my soul, the kind of tingling one feels in anticipation of something wonderful happening very soon.

Having been hospitalized for years between America and China for treatment of the severe juvenile rheumatoid arthritis that has made a home within my body since infancy, receiving education—the knowledge of life—for the very first time was a thrill for me; no longer was I lying on my hospital bed daydreaming about going to school and reading.

My eyes relished the sight of the words as I pronounced them aloud. I smiled to myself when I was able to read a complete sentence, then an entire paragraph.

A couple of hours flew by before my mother opened the door to my room, and I greeted her with a big grin. "I can read much of the book!" I declared.

I wondered, when I might catch up to those students who had already had five years of schooling. The words I had just learned were all that I knew. I had no idea from where rain comes or why we see a rainbow after a refreshing rain.

Wanting to learn as much as I could as quickly as possible, I absorbed all that was taught in class, and mostly self-taught myself how to read; like Cookie Monster, I devoured one book after another as though they were chocolate chip cookies, yet always hungered for more.

After about 180 days of attendance, my special education teacher told my mother: "She's ready to go to a regular sixth grade class, and she'll do very well in it."

Eight years later, I reminisced about those 180 days as I sat on the stage before hundreds of people. It was my high school graduation ceremony, and I was a student speaker who excitedly awaited my turn to speak.

My mother held the microphone for me when my turn arrived. "Good evening, my fellow graduates," I began. "My name is Shirley Cheng. It is certainly an honor in speaking to welcome and congratulate every one of you tonight! First, I would like to take this opportunity to thank those people who have made it possible for me to be here tonight: my beloved mom Juliet, (who is here beside me, holding the microphone), who has been giving me unwavering love, support, and encouragement; Mrs. Shapley, who took the time to personally administer the test to me; and every single teacher who has given me the treasure of knowledge. I have no words to describe how grand I feel right now, so I'm not even going to try. I have encountered numerous barriers in getting an education due to my physical disabilities, but I still strove to prevail, to achieve my heart's desire." Several camera lights flashed before my eyes. The audience applauded when I shared with them my life story.

"Unfortunately, I lost my eyesight towards the end of my sophomore year in high school. So, I received home-tutoring instead, but was unable to accumulate enough credits to get a regents high school diploma. Thus, I received a high school equivalency diploma instead, and for which I am very, very, very grateful! I took the GED test using cassette tapes and a tape recorder. I did everything in my head without seeing anything, including math calculations and graphs. I also recorded my essay on the tape recorder. And I scored over 3200." Another round of applause broke out. When the noise died down, I continued.

"Well, all that's left to say now is that I am thankful to be here, knowing I can take the next step of my journey. I want to congratulate every one of you for having come this far with your ambitions. Give yourself a pat on the back, and know that whatever you have your heart set on, you shall achieve it, and no matter what hardship you may face, you shall prevail. Be strong, listen hard to the voice calling from your heart. Do what your heart desires, and if anything or anyone gets in your way, turn your head and go in another direction to achieve your goals. Thank you and have a great night all!" I flashed the audience a big smile.

I could barely hear my mother over the

thunderous applause as she said, "They're all standing up!" Cameras flashed from every corner, bathing me in radiance.

After the speeches, the special recognition awards were handed out to ten students, including me, for scoring over 3,000 on the GED exam. "Your speech was great," commented the lady, while handing me my award. Then the audience cheered for each of the ninety-four students as they received their diplomas.

After the ceremony ended, several people, mostly parents from the audience, came up to me. "That's a wonderful speech. It was the best I've heard in a long time," remarked an official from the school district.

"Your speech touched me. It almost made me cry," commented an audience member.

More compliments flew my way as my mother pushed me out of the auditorium. A few people stretched out their hands for me to shake. "I would like to take your picture," said one gentleman. I gladly posed for the shot, my mind drifting back to those unforgettable 180 days.

Yes, those 180 days were truly special education; they opened the door to a whole new world for me. It wasn't just a moment's pleasure, but an everlasting treasure of self-fulfillment and endless opportunities to great success. I smile each time I recollect those days and how far I have come, from learning to read an entire book for the first time to publishing my own books.

Sing Me a Song

Sing me a song
I may build a dream on
Create notes soothing and light
To the melodies, my heart shall dance in flight
Sensational delights please do bring
For my heart to do a swing
The notes will travel all around
Flowing gracefully with no bounds
In grace, for all souls to marvel
Even a smile it'll bestow upon grumpy
Mr. Harvel

A Moment with Shirley

You are the creator of your sunshine and the bringer of your storms.

Happy Winds

Happily winds sing
Tickling green leaves to dances
Stirring grass whistles

White Umbrellas

Wee white umbrellas
Puffy dandelion seeds
Swirling in the wind

Shimmering Feathers

Shimmering feathers
Of ocean blue and sea green
Hummingbirds display

Crystalline Flowers

Crystalline flowers
Alight on frozen mirrors
Forming white castles

Upside Down Meals

Food falls over heads
Drool drips up their cheeks — how sloths
Love meals upside down!

Veil of Willows

Strands of willow hair
Veil black swan couple in a
Secluded lagoon

The Summer Breeze

Oh, how I love the summer breeze
As I dance about in its arms!
The tunes it sings to me
Makes my spirit spring with glee
Here and there, my heart skips a beat
In rapture, how it does swing!
The delights, the music brings forth
For me to share endlessly henceforth
My arms open, I collect the gems
These treasures I will send on with a kiss
So all may dance as happily
And sing their songs so freely!

Midsummer's Blue Sky

Clouds float peacefully
Across the endless stretch of
Midsummer's blue sky

Love on Midsummer's Nights

On midsummer's nights
Crickets carry sweet tunes far
To where lovers sigh

Wrath of Nature

Dark green skies spinning
Wild black twirling winds wherein
Lives wrath of nature

Where the Old Oak Stands

Where the old oak stands
The orange sun places a gentle hand
Upon the sleeping soul, gently stroking
Atop the spirit the sunlight cloaking
A blanket to awaken the quiet soul
Patching up the darkness of the tiny hole
Wherein the heart irregularly beats
The coldness, the sun to defeat

Tumbling Leaves

Slowly, leaves tumble
From home, greeting vibrant friends
For a gentle rest

The Red Silver Fir

The red silver fir
Yonder the quiet valleys
Peacefully asleep

Meadow of Cotton Balls

Along green meadows
Hopping cotton balls dotting
White rabbits frolic

Praying Mantis

On a cloistered leaf
Rests a mantis, forelimbs raised
For what does it pray?

Red, Orange Leaves

Red, orange leaves float
In clusters on still waters
From trees, leaves collect

Playful Rays

Rays playfully tease
Foamy flowers atop waves
Sending all aglow

The Jewel from Heavenly Father

1st place winning entry in the 2nd annual Be the Star You Are! National writing contest in January 2006

Heavenly Father bestowed upon me the most precious jewel on the day my life began. This treasure has shone endless light upon me, bringing unconditional love, unwavering support, overflowing happiness, and the softest serenity to my life. I have never felt empty or alone, as I know the gem has me wrapped in its warm blanket, protecting me from the darkest corners of the world. Although twenty-two years have flown by, battling through wind and storms, its sublimity is undaunted, and not a speck of dust has ruined its beauty. It continues to shimmer, not flinching from any dirt or mud. I always have it near me; if it is physically away, it is always locked safely in my heart.

That diamond is my beloved mother Juliet Cheng, a beautiful woman in every sense of the word. When she smiles, the world lights up alongside her. When she cries, the days seem to dim in sorrow. Together, my mother and I have shared laughter and tears; the best of times and the worst of times. We have fought as a team with our swords of justice.

We have conquered fiery oceans and thorny jungles and come out with stars in our arms. She has climbed all the high mountains with me, supporting and encouraging me every step of the way. She has carried me on dangerous roads and saved my life numerous times from the grasp of death. I would have been long gone if it had not been for her invincible stamina and courage to fight for my life to the end.

My mother has done all this while battling her own horrendous illnesses. But she keeps moving forward, never abandoning me nor faltering in any way. Her light shines ever so bright, never dimming as the years pass us by. She does everything in her power to keep me well and happy. Her love for me is "higher than the sky and deeper than the ocean." With her love always within me, I feel all the wonders of sensations. I am a billionaire though my pockets are empty. I have all the riches in the world: love, happiness, peace, security, and support. What more is there to life than those pearls of the universe? She gives me all of those treasures without expecting anything in return. She is my life, and I give her all I can offer — my love, heart, and soul.

She is as gentle as a summer's breeze, but the lioness in her jumps out when she defends and protects me from the harshness of the world. Her wit is as sharp as a sword, and she is unafraid to use it against injustice whenever it tries to harm me. Not only is she a protector of mine—she embraces everyone, but the world has not always returned her hugs. Nevertheless, she remains a lover, never sour with anyone.

No one is able to separate us. They may separate us physically (as the world has done several times), but we can never be spiritually separated. We live within each other's hearts; if we are oceans away, we will still be near to each other. She calls me her star, and I, too, call her my star. We are binary stars, ever revolving around each other, never drifting apart. She will never be absent of her fiery glow, and I will forever shine by her side. As long as there is life, there will be her love and mine.

A Moment with Shirley

If you have eyesight, use it to
see far and wide.
If you work with hands, lend
one to help the one in need.
If you travel by foot, walk
down the street to help the
elderly cross.
And if you have lips, curve
them into a smile to turn
someone's frown upside down.

With You by My Side

With you by my side
I will always sigh
To the treasures we share
Day or night
The days may be stormy
But your light will conquer
All that we may face
Like my knight in shining armor

The road we travel
Indeed is narrow and long!
At every corner, darkness lurks
Yet the joy you bring forth
Turns the journey into delight
A memory to savor
For till the time ends
I shall forever be thanking you

Glorious Stars

Bright glorious stars
Secretly winking to say
Burn with love of me

Black and White Pair

Black and white pair swims
In elegant harmony
Two loons in sweet love

Silly Peek-A-Boo

Green head popping out
Playing silly peek-a-boo
Then inside it goes

Veil of Waterfalls

Waterfalls veil a
Mysterious world behind
Cascading curtains

Tumbling Waterfalls

Waterfall tumbles
Showering crystalline rocks
With silky touches

Wing Dance

Wing to wing they dance
Twirling to dance of delight
Among puffs of clouds

Twilight Serenade

Far and wide, the music flows
In between grasses, through deep forests
To the notes, crickets sing along
As the meadow thrives all aglow
To the melodies, all creatures sing
As the last ray dies away
For the orange sun has gone to rest
And in its place, the moon awakes

Under the wide misty skies
The twilight serenade has begun
All around, lights flash
In unison with flowing melodies
The tunes, the winds carry them afar
Reaching all the midnight fauna
Beating to their stirring hearts
Their waking spirits to bear the songs on

A Moment with Shirley

Scorn not those with no feet,
for birds do not scorn you who
have no wings.

Twilight Greeting

Early birds, night owls
Briefly greet one another
In misty twilight

Midnight Ghostly Lights

Ghostly lights flicker
In the silence of midnight
Turning on, off, on

Sleepy Spells

Sleepy spells owls cast
Carried by winds deep into
Awaiting darkness

That Secretive Grin

This poem is dedicated to the late "Crocodile Hunter" Steve Irwin, who left this world on September 4, 2006, while doing what he dearly loved. May God bless his passionate soul!

Grinning in secret thought
The crocodile trudges ashore
His tail swinging to and fro
To every step of power he takes
His long claws, he proudly shows
The imprints they leave mark grand entrance
The narrow eyes, they scan the distance
Zooming in on the slightest movements
Along the shore, he roams for venture
Bearing the grin that promises adventure
Critters look on with reverence
To this mighty king of the shore
Overhead, gulls screech in a taunt
Minding them not, the croc leisurely treads on
As the sun sets, he thinks it's about time
To depart to his much-missed watery realm
So back home, he carries that secretive grin
For, tonight, he knows, he will explore again
No wonder his heart is so content
To live in two such wondrous worlds!

Weeping Ocean

Ocean splashing waves
Hiding deep sorrow in depths
Forever weeping

Moaning Winds

Winds moaning in pain
Disturbing tree limbs in sleep
For consolation

Seashell Sighing

Delicate seashell
Sighs to the beating heart of
Ocean waves splashing

Withering White

White roses wither
Sorrowfully of love lost
To blossoming red

Kiss of King Cobra

King Cobra snaking
Up to a nest of hatchlings
For a kiss of death

Guilty Mockingbirds

Mockingbirds mimic
Neighboring feathered friends while
Feigning innocence

The School People Crave

What would you say if I asked you to return to school? "Been there, done that"? How would you like to go to the largest school with the longest classes and the most homework assignments in the world? Sounds awful? Then think again...

It is a huge school with countless courses to graduate and hours and hours of homework to complete, at times making time appear short, although everyone gets varying amounts of time to complete a variety of tasks. No two people share the exact assignments, but everyone shares a common goal: to graduate with honors. And it is possible for everyone to achieve that if each one studies hard and completes their work in a responsible manner — and no A's or even B's are required!

In this school, there is no turning back, as you cannot fail. Sure, you can be held back a grade, but you will have endless opportunities to learn from your mistakes and earn a diploma for each accomplishment. For each step forward, you will receive points that build up, making you smarter and wiser as you obtain knowledge from the world around you. There is no going back, only forward, as teachers in this school prohibit people from returning to kindergarten.

The teachers are not intimidating in any

way, for they are the students and the students are the teachers. Yes, you will teach and guide your fellow students. Teachers can make mistakes, but they do not worry because their classmates can show them the way. You will be able to set good examples while you learn and do your own work, thus everyone benefits in this school environment. The teachers continually learn new materials as they teach, so no one declares that they have finished learning.

When you arrive at your graduation ceremony, you anticipate holding a multitude of awards in your hands, but the most rewarding award is the feeling that you know you have done your very best. You receive self-fulfillment when you say, "I've had fun achieving my goals. I've had a blast making a difference to the world." During the ceremony, as tears of happiness and contentment are shed by yourself and fellow graduates, you receive your awards as the crowd cheers. Yes, go get that "Outstanding Award in Best Mother" and "Excellence in Receiving Straight A's in Love."

So, if you had the option of attending this school, would you? Would you want to be given endless opportunities to achieve? Would you like to use your mistakes to your advantage? I know I would. I would want to graduate with high honors after falling down over and over again only to find another chance to pick myself up to change and learn.

Do I hear a yes? Well, then I have the

best news for you: each and every one of us is in this school, including yours truly, so there is no need to panic if you have not enrolled. Where is this school anyway, and how do you know you are actually in the school, you ask? The school is in the comfort of your own home, or at work or at the doctor's office. You know you are attending this school because of the endless opportunities you have to thrive and learn.

The school is life. So, pick up that pen of responsibility and that paper of patience, and get your current assignments done so that you can receive your next diploma! And do not forget to give yourself a pat on the back when you graduate with high honors.

A Moment with Shirley

The best winners in life are the best losers.

Will I Still Feel It?

Tell me, when the dark steals in
When curtains have fallen
And the noises silenced
Will I still feel it?

Do you know, if my road a mountain has blocked
My view a fog has clouded
And I stumble a step or two
Will I still feel it?

What if the sky decides to cry
Winds begin a storm
And trees go up in flames
Will I still feel it?

Will I still feel the wings
That lift me high
And helped me through hard times?

Yes, the answer blows in the wind
The wings will beat through the future storm
Out of darkness into the light
Forevermore I will feel it

Cool April Showers

Cool April showers
Lightly kissing sprouting buds
Blessing healthy green

Rain's Masterpiece

Rain washing blue skies
Painting a masterpiece of
Seven bright colors

Shameless Rooster

Raising its head high
Proud rooster shamelessly calls
Waking sun's slumber

Hunger of Venus Flytrap

Red Venus Flytrap
Quietly waits, mouth widely
Open in hunger

Darting Blue Shadows

Blue shadows flicker
In the depths of oceans, fish
Dart between seaweed

Ocean Sighs

Oh, little seashell
The essence of ocean sighs
You capture so well!

When Your Spirit Is Blue

When your spirit is blue
Raise your head to the sun
Bright upon the clear blue sky
Feel the rays shine through
To wash the blueness away

If ever your spirit is green
Open your ears and listen
The songs winds sing to you
Feel it touch your soul
To gently take away the hurt

When you see a spirit in blue
Put your arms around the one
In need of a warm embrace
To throw away the sorrow
As the sun has showed you how

And if you ever see a spirit in green
Whistle a tune from your heart
To carry away the hurt
To far, far away places
As the winds have taught you how

A Moment with Shirley

One who frets over the future has not learned from the past.

Hot Pink Flamingo

Hot pink flamingo
Preens bright plumage, balancing
On one slender leg

Festive Motif

Rainbow-colored lights
Flashing in festive motif
On tall evergreens

Migrating V

The large V arrows
Southward silently; a group
Of geese migrating

Awake!

Awake!
The rainbow lies just yonder
The new day with hope anew
Overflowing with all things of wonder
Treasures to spread to quite a few
But go there quickly you must
For shadows will come in time
To hide all that shines under dust
Awake your spirit while gems shine in their prime

Tickle Me Not

Tiny black legs move
In rhythmic waves; oh, tickle
me not, millipede!

Lullaby Whistle

Gentle night breezes
Whistle soothing lullaby
Putting souls to rest

Sliding in Tuxedos

Upon white bellies
Into waters penguins slide
Dressed in tuxedos

Rise!

Rise!
Many joys have been left un-enjoyed
Their delights never before felt
Rise to feel the treasures
For the pleasures are beyond measures

Rise!
Do a little dance
Swing to the music within
To the lyrics, sing along
Happiness is where your soul belongs

A Moment with Shirley

Weep not when the sun has set,
for it has gone to warm the
other world, and shall return in
less than a day.

Weep not when the rain has
fallen, for it feeds souls in
thirst, and washes all dirt
away.

Weep not when flowers have
withered, for they have left
their young to grow, and have
enriched the soil with love.

About the Author

Shirley Cheng, born in 1983, a blind and physically disabled motivational speaker, poet, author of five books, and contributing author of seven books, is a miracle survivor with tremendous talents, an exceptional, tenacious spirit, and a colorful personality. She was diagnosed with severe juvenile rheumatoid arthritis at only eleven months old. She spent her early years in constant pain, confined to a wheelchair, and was hospitalized for many years while living between China and America until 1994. Unable to receive any form of education until her health was stabilized, Shirley started attending school at age eleven in a special education class in elementary school. Back then, she knew very little English, and her knowledge on other subjects was non-existent. Miraculously, she mastered grade level in all areas after approximately 180 days of attendance, and she immediately entered a regular sixth grade class in middle school.

Shirley has a voracious appetite for books, reading an average of six hundred pages (three books) daily, and has read over a total of two thousand books. Since sixth grade, she has received 100 on every NYS essay test, and stayed at the top of the class ever since. She was awarded for achieving the highest grade of 97 in Earth science in her eighth grade class. She was the Student of the Year and the

Student of the Month, as well as a three-time winner of the National Reflections Program in visual arts. She has a passion for writing both prose and poetry. Two of her writings were published when she was fourteen and fifteen. One of her short stories, *Mary Miller, the Elusive Lady*, received Honorable Mention and was published by the *Poughkeepsie Journal* in 1997, and her poem, *The Colors of the Rainbow*, earned merit status and was published in *Celebrate! New York Young Poets Speak Out* in 1999.

Shirley was a contributor to her high school newspaper, providing artwork in tenth grade. She received a standing ovation when she delivered a speech as a candidate for student body vice president in ninth grade.

When her eyesight began to deteriorate at the beginning of tenth grade, she had to use two magnifying glasses, holding one on top of the other, on enlarged print to do her work throughout the year, including the artwork she provided for the school newspaper. In classes, she learned only by listening to her teachers, even with chemistry and math, as she was unable to see the blackboard; still she maintained excellent grades.

Unfortunately, Shirley completely lost her vision in April of tenth grade. She then received home-tutoring, and successfully completed all her schoolwork by using cassette tapes and tape recorders. She wrote and balanced long chemistry formulas and equations without vision or Braille (she cannot use Braille because of her severe arthritis). Her high school overall average was 97 (a 3.9 GPA without any advanced placement classes). But Shirley could not accumulate enough credits to receive a high school diploma from her school due to her vision loss. In 2002, she received her high school equivalency diploma. She took the entire GED test, including mathematical calculations, graphs, and an essay, in her head, and received a special recognition award for scoring an exceptionally high 3280. She was a student speaker at the GED graduation ceremony, and received a standing ovation for her speech.

Shirley became an author at age twenty, completing three books within one year. She wrote her books using a screen reader on her computer, typing with her two index fingers at the speed of about sixty words per minute. She successfully completed every self-publishing task, including formatting her manuscripts, on her own.

Waking Spirit: Prose & Poems the Spirit Sings is comprised of selected pieces written when Shirley was twenty-three, except for *The Jewel from Heavenly Father*, which she wrote at the age of twenty-two. In January 2006, this piece tied for 1st place in the second annual Be the Star You Are! National writing contest founded by Cynthia Brian. Shirley's winning entry is dedicated to her beloved mother Juliet Cheng, the cornerstone and light of her life. In the following January, Shirley received

Honorable Mention in the same contest for her essay, *I Hold the Power*, her personal story of overcoming blindness.

Shirley has an immense passion for life and is full of life and vigor. Despite her severe disabilities, Shirley has striven to overcome overwhelming obstacles and she is living the life she loves, while she empowers, inspires, and motivates others to do the same.

Shirley was brought up in a very simple, single-parent, Chinese-speaking family with no influence on education. She pursues her education on her own. She has extraordinary goals with the aspiration of attending college at Harvard University, where she plans to earn doctorates in microbiology, zoology, astronomy, physiology, and pathology, after a successful eye surgery.

Shirley is a true magical gift, a star with endless shine.

Shirley As an Advocate

Shirley is also an advocate of parental rights in children's medical care, and aide/caregiver monitoring and screening for students with special needs and disabled people.

As a parental rights advocate, she wants to help today's loving parents protect and keep custody of their children. "In America, parents risk losing custody of their children forever if they disagree with doctors' recommended treatments, or even when they want a second opinion," says Shirley, a survivor of two custody battles her mother Juliet Cheng had with doctors. Shirley adds, "When doctors ask yes or no, parents should have the right to say no."

Shirley's last case made international headlines in 1990; Juliet appeared on *CBS This Morning* with Paula Zahn as she fought to save Shirley's life and prevent her from receiving the harmful treatment recommended by her doctor in Connecticut.

Shirley promotes aide advocacy for the disabled because she was mistreated and abused by one-on-one aides when she attended school. "The trouble with uncaring aides actually lies with the authorities," she says. "If they had listened to my complaints and kept a close watch on the aides, I wouldn't have gone through all the suffering."

Spotlight Reviews

An inspirational miscellany from one of the braver souls on the planet. The author of a number of works in genres ranging from memoir to short fiction to poetry, this motivational speaker is seldom at a loss for words to celebrate life and promote her indefatigable character. Here, Cheng collects a menagerie of lyrics, haiku, short personal essays and even briefer aphoristic words to live by—all on the theme of leaping over seemingly insurmountable hurdles, a subject with which this author is well-acquainted. Though plagued from infancy with near-fatal juvenile rheumatoid arthritis and then blindness as a teenager, Cheng continues to tackle on the page all life has to offer, enlisting but her two index fingers, the aid of a screen-reader program that reads back what she's composed and her indomitable will.

Cheng's prose statements detail a few of her tribulations, offering philosophical insights on suffering, though never with a hint of self-pity; her poems, particularly the vivid haiku, turn more to objects of the natural world that delight her.

For those ready to be eased of their burdens, Cheng provides a lift.
— *Kirkus Discoveries*

This book is an amazing read by an amazing person. While shops and shelves are piled with inspirational and self-help books written by people with disabilities, only luck can lead the reader to an author capable of transporting them to a world outside the normal and understood. Shirley Cheng is one of these lucky finds, driven as she is to help others understand the lives of the disabled.

Cheng is one person who has never allowed her differences to dictate her attitude towards life. She not only appreciates life as a gift, but expresses gratitude to her mother for her positive outlook on life, and to the existence with which her Heavenly Father has blessed her. No matter what, Cheng views her life as an opportunity to make the most of, and views her differences as giving her a unique outlook on life.

Waking Spirit is a collection of poetry of different types including haiku, quotations and essays that embody Cheng's positive attitude towards life and strategies for dealing with adversity. Her writing is very accessible and enjoyable as she "shows without telling," without arrogance or preachiness.

This book is an expression of joy, of wonder, and of passion for life. It teaches simple truths and lifelong lessons that are often overlooked in the current complex world.

—*Karen L. Sadler*
ForeWord Magazine CLARION Reviews

> Warm, luminous, and an easy pleasure.

— *Christina Francine, Midwest Book Review*

If you enjoy reading the thoughts of someone who has confronted her own mortality, pain, and flawed body at a young age to emerge as a spiritual champion who "sees" the beauty around her, you'll love this book. One of Shirley Cheng's inspirations is that there are always those who have more problems than she does. If you draw from that lesson, you'll be counting your blessings all day long . . . and seeing the spiritual beauty of life, as well.

In the essays in *Waking Spirit*, Ms. Cheng recounts her spiritual journey in a way that would move a boulder to dance.

Her happiness is so pervasive that you may at first not be able to tune into it. Through a combination of essays, aphorisms, poems and haiku, you'll find yourself moving up in spiritual blessedness from this uplifting volume.

— *Donald Mitchell*
Founder of The Billionaire Entrepreneurs' Master Mind

I had the privilege of reading *Waking Spirit* by Shirley Cheng. I say a privilege because she is that rare someone who has been able to rise above the trials of life. Her spirit shines through every word, lifting your heart and making you dance beside her. Her poetry paints a picture and you are there. Her piercing

insights belie her young age and you feel the wisdom in her words. Her gifts are boundless and take us all to a loftier place we can only dream about. Thank you Shirley for letting us dance with you.
— *Robbie Miles*
Brush Artist and Teacher

Shirley Cheng creates beautiful worlds of inspiration by focusing on a positive outlook. Her wisdom and captivating writing style reveals a rare beauty of the heart. Humorous haiku blends effortlessly with devotional selections as quotes sing a wisdom we want to hear and live.

This book takes you on journeys of spirit, where you feel nurtured and loved in this world of magical joy. Her visions of delicate wonder are a warm soothing revelation.

I can highly recommend *Waking Spirit* as well as *Dance with Your Heart: Tales and Poems That The Heart Tells*.

The positive energy in Shirley Cheng's books is refreshing, real and inspiring. I hope you will invite her writing into your heart to experience the beauty of love's transforming energy.
— *The Rebecca Review*
Amazon.com Top 10 Reviewer

Constantly our Great Creator blesses us with a gift to remind us why life is so special

and worth hanging around for. Hellen Keller was one of those gifts, and now the world is lucky enough to have blind and disabled Shirley Cheng take up Helen's gauntlet, and remind us of how special life can be and what a courageous survivor is all about. Shirley Cheng's new book *Waking Spirit* is a masterpiece and you would be making a wise decision to take time to read its poignant contents. Shirley proves the motto of the world Positive Thinkers club holds water through the centuries of time. "The Positive Thinker sees the invisible, feels the intangible and achieves the impossible. That is what Shirley is all about!
— *Ken Bossone*
President of World Positive Thinkers Club

    Shirley is an excellent thought provoking writer and poet with a charm and intelligence that would make anyone envious. Shirley's ability to see life in such a positive way has left a lasting impression on many of her readers, myself included. Her inspiration and never ending strive to see all good in life is rare and commendable and should be used as a definite positive thought when one feels that things are just not fair in their lives. Her age and illness has never stood in her way of succeeding and embracing everything that life has to offer.
— *Dorothy Lafrinere*
WomensSelfEsteem.com

Shirley Cheng presents stirring medley of brief individual composition, haiku, lyrical offering and discourse. Well written, adeptly fashioned this poet presents keenly focused love of life, sentiment and enthusiasm. Cheng's work is sure to entrance readers who love poetry as well as captivate those who do not care so much for lyrical form. *Waking Spirit* is filled with passion, happiness and joy of life as bard Cheng sets down her feelings and feeling for the life she cannot see around her. As we read the writers lovely words we are drawn into her world of joy and happiness and forget that she is wheelchair bound and not able to see what we can run and touch and view.

Waking Spirit is a work for all who want something to read and re read. Because the work is not a 'story book' it is nice to carry in the car for the odd moment to have a quick read as you wait for the kid's dental appointment to end, or the train to pass. *Waking Spirit* will make a nice addition to the home library, high school classroom book shelf and the gift 'tuck in' for Mom, favorite aunty or birthday girl sister.

— *Molly Martin*
The Compulsive Reader

Shirley's poetry, which spans a variety of meters, tones, and topics, is always eloquent and heartfelt. For me, the highlights were the short and simple poems that described daily scenes, endowing them with a new sense of

importance. The way Shirley cherished the small pleasures in life encouraged me to slow down and enjoy a trail of ants, or the birds flying overhead. I feel that she has helped me open my eyes to a different world, one that is intricately laced with simple joys. Additionally, I particularly liked inserts of *A Moment With Shirley*, which are gems of comfort, advice, and inspiration. It felt like I had a best friend, providing me with encouragement.
— *Jennifer Tao, 17*
Be the Star You Are!

Lest you think that the best writing is by the best-known authors, the best written piece in the book is by Shirley Cheng, whose work you may not know yet. . . but you should. The title? *Dance with Your Heart: How to Befriend Your Heart and the World around You.*
— *Donald Mitchell*
Founder of The Billionaire Entrepreneurs' Master Mind, Strategic Management professor, bestselling author and consultant (Excerpted from his review for 101 Great Ways to Improve Your Life, Volume 2)

Other Books by Shirley

Shirley is also the author of:
- *Daring Quests of Mystics*
ISBN-13: 978-1-4116-5664-2
- *The Revelation of a Star's Endless Shine: A Young Woman's Autobiography of 20-Year Victories over Victimization*
ISBN-13: 978-0-6151-5044-4
- *Dance with Your Heart: Tales and Poems That the Heart Tells*, a collection of inspirational and fantasy prose (fairy tales, fables, and myths) and poetry for the heart from the heart
ISBN-13: 978-1-4116-1858-9
- *Parental Rights in Children's Medical Care – Where Is Our Freedom to Say No? A Look at the Injustice of the American Medical System*
ISBN-13: 978-0-6151-4994-3

With highly acclaimed experts like Dr. Wayne Dyer, Tony Robbins, and Brian Tracy, Shirley co-authored *Wake Up…Live the Life You Love: Finding Your Life's Passion, Second Edition* (ISBN-13: 9781933063058), an installment in the bestselling *Wake Up…Live the Life You Love* series; she is also the co-author of *101 Great Ways to Improve Your Life, Volume 2* (ISBN-13: 9780974567273), along with leading experts like Jack Canfield, John Gray, Richard Carlson, Alan Cohen, Bob Proctor, et al.

Book Awards

Waking Spirit is the recipient of:

- 2009 Mom's Choice Awards
- The Avatar Award for Spiritual Excellence in Literature (2008)
- Best book in three categories of Reader Views 2007 Annual Literary Awards: First Place in Poetry Nonfiction, and Second Place in both New Age Nonfiction and Spirituality/Inspiration
- Finalist in the national Indie Excellence 2007 Book Awards
- Honorable Mention in the 2007 New York Book Festival Competition in Poetry
- Honorable Mention in the 2007 DIY Book Festival in Poetry

Embrace Ultra-Ability! Wisdom, Insight & Motivation from the Blind Who Sees Far and Wide is the recipient of:

- Nine Parent to Parent Adding Wisdom Awards, including Adult Health & Well-being, Books – Inspirational/Christian, Gifts for Mom, Gifts for Dad, and Unique Products
- 2008 Reader Views Literary Awards – Honorable Mention for Body/Mind/Spirit
- Finalist in the 2008 Next Generation Indie Book Awards in Motivational
- Finalist in the National Best Books 2008 Awards in Philosophy

Shirley on the WWW

Visit Shirley on the Web at http://www.shirleycheng.com to learn more about her, her books, listen to some of her radio show interviews, e-mail her, and subscribe to her monthly newsletter, *Inspiration from a Blind*, to receive words of inspiration, special news and events information, and exclusive offers for members. Her newsletter issues are archived on her blog, http://blog.shirleycheng.com to which people can subscribe via e-mail or RSS.

Personalized autographed copies of all of Shirley's books are available from her website.

Her books are also available through Ingram, from Amazon.com (and their international sites) and BN.com, and also available through brick-and-mortar Waldenbooks and Borders stores.

Shirley is available for interviews, speaking engagements, book signings, and inspirational events.

Support a Good Cause

Some of the proceeds from the sale of this book, *Waking Spirit: Prose & Poems the Spirit Sings*, will go to Christian Blind Mission International and Be the Star You Are!

Christian Blind Mission International (CBMI), based in Germany with affiliate offices in ten countries, is the oldest and largest ministry with the primary purpose of improving the quality of life for the blind and disabled in 113 developing countries, providing preventative, medical, rehabilitative and educational services in more than one thousand projects. Their aid is available to all people regardless of religion, nationality, race, or gender.
http://www.cbmi.org (International)
http://www.cbmiusa.org (USA)
http://www.cbmicanada.org (Canada)

"Being blind or disabled is already hard enough without having to endure the suffering resulting from economic barriers. I have always wished to help anyone in need, and this is my chance to do so. I hope people will support me in this good cause," says Shirley.

Be the Star You Are! is a not-for-profit 501(c)(3) corporation founded by Cynthia Brian in 1999 that collects and distributes books and other positive media to youth at risk as a way to raise their life skills and self esteem.
http://www.bethestaryouare.org

www.ingramcontent.com/pod-product-compliance
Lightning Source LLC
LaVergne TN
LVHW011423080426
835512LV00005B/228